D0325864

THE CASE

of the

MISSING CUTLERY

A LEADERSHIP COURSE *for* THE RISING STAR

-----

by

KEVIN ALLEN

Bestselling author of *The Hidden Agenda*

To Joan M. Allen
The lady who keeps our ship afloat.

———————————

First published by Bibliomotion, Inc.

33 Manchester Road
Brookline, MA 02446
Tel: 617-934-2427
www.bibliomotion.com

Printed in the United States of America

ISBN print: 978-1-62956-024-3
ISBN ebook: 978-1-62956-025-0
ISBN enhanced ebook: 978-1-62956-026-7

Contents

Introduction

"Well, kid, welcome to the club. You are now dinner conversation."

These words, said to me when I was promoted to my first management role at Marriott International, rang in my ears. I was an excited twenty-two-year-old former floor mopper who would now be a shift manager, with several dozen people working for me.

Actually, I was terrified.

I couldn't get my mind off the idea that I would be dinner conversation. What would the people I managed say about me? What should I say to them? How would I get them to do as I asked? They all had far more experience doing their jobs, and the large majority were far older than I—some were even old enough to be my parents. Surely they would see that I didn't have a clue what to do.

Years later, when I was made executive vice president at McCann Erickson Worldwide, I felt the same twinge of anxiety. Soon I came to realize that the gift of human empathy, which had guided me through those early days at Marriott, would allow me to steer literally thousands of people to row in the direction of McCann Erickson's future.

As my career has progressed, I've learned things the hard way, through trial and error…mostly error. Through it all, I came to realize people don't follow you because of a chain of command, or because of discipline, orderliness, or even intimidation. They follow you because of who you are; because you have come to understand the deep desires and hopes of your people; and because, by connecting with them, you have created a culture and a common cause they believe in.

So that dinner conversation can go one of two ways. Around

their dining tables, your people could be grousing bitterly, "Do you know what he did to us today?" Conversely, with excitement in their voices, they could be saying, "Guess what we did today!" The difference lies in your ability to reach your people on a purely emotional level. As a leader, you do not preside or command; instead you float, buoyant, because the people you lead believe you should. They reward your generosity, your belief in them, and your ability to galvanize them toward a common purpose by believing in you.

To be sure, decisiveness is a requisite of leadership, but it is not what inspires people to make you float. They see, through your empathy, that you give them as high a priority as you do yourself and that you have created a culture and climate in which they can flourish.

When I got into the business world I quickly saw what appeared to be "rules" for leadership. From the oft-mimicked behaviors I observed, it seemed that success belonged to the swaggering "tough guy" types who ate bowls of nails for breakfast, and who bellowed orders and made clear who was boss. I quickly took inventory of myself; as a somewhat soft-spoken, altogether emotional person, I deduced that I did not possess the requisite skills for leadership.

Take heart. Success didn't—and doesn't—depend on a tough-as-nails bearing.

As a kid from the wrong side of the tracks, I learned from a very young age to play the hand I was dealt. I couldn't "command" my way into being followed I would have to encourage followers to join me. Blessed with a highly intuitive nature, I could easily relate to people—I understood how they felt and could instinctively zero in on their unstated desires. Quietly, I would set out to find a way to connect with these people and bring them together toward some amazing end. I saw management not as a practice but as a journey that we all traveled together. I realized quickly that the way to achieve a something great was not just to manage but also to ignite.

Leadership is an act of human empathy and generosity of spirit. When people know you understand their hopes and desires, and you make your connection clear to them and show confidence that you as a community can get there, they'll follow you anywhere.

Why This Book?

After a thirty-year career, first at Marriott International then in the global advertising business, I came to a realization. I discovered that the joy of my life and career was no longer my own success, but rather seeing the up-and-coming leadership of the company succeed. With company turnarounds, mayoral elections, and the now-famous "Priceless" campaign for MasterCard and many others behind me, I realized that the thrill for me was not another account win; it was picking up the phone to hear the excited voices of a young team I coached exclaiming, "We won it!"

What a joy.

I formed my company, re:kap, three years ago to help people and companies achieve what they seek. Increasingly, we receive a good deal of correspondence from frontline leaders asking how they can lead their people and their company to win in the marketplace. These requests have come particularly from practicing managers and leaders who are confronted in their organizations with the challenges and difficulties of leading their teams. I created The Buoyant Leader as an ecosystem—made up of this book, online instruction, and community support—to help leaders on their heroic journey to survive and thrive. So, in effect, this program is for you.

Mentorship is much of what this program, and my company, is about. Our mission is to inspire you to set exciting ambitions and reach them confidently; to encourage you to know that the very person you are—as you are—can get you to your goals; and to equip you with the tools and practices to deal with the management issues you may face along the way.

What You'll Take Away

The Case of the Missing Cutlery is designed with several goals in mind:

1. To provide a proven treatise on the concepts of contemporary leadership you can apply right away.
2. To outfit you with practical, easily implemented methods and tools to use in your leadership journey.
3. To structure a "course" with tasks and applications you and others can employ in the context of your working environment.
4. To equip you with an in-the-minute reference guide you can refer to when you confront new and challenging leadership situations.

How It Is Organized

The Case of the Missing Cutlery is organized in two parts:

I. The Case Many books and articles on achieving success in business rightly cite such stellar successes as Apple, GE, and other luminary organizations. When I was coming up in business, both on the job and at graduate school, these notable cases taught me much, but I confess that at times in my day-to-day business life I struggled to see how Steve Jobs's or Jack Welch's lofty exploits correlated with my role as an entry-level shift manager. I spent much of my formative business years in a virtual wilderness, and, with no role models in my family, I discovered everything through trial and error. So when I give examples, I do not draw on the loftier cases in my experience, but on the simplest, and probably most profound.

II. A Course in Buoyancy Leadership is not a static thing. It is neither sitting nor presiding—it's going somewhere. Leadership is a journey toward a fantastic goal. So in this spirit, this section takes you on a hero's journey and breaks down the elements in a leadership path. I'll connect these principles and tools to "The Case" to help your practical application. It's laid out in a course framework, with tasks for you to apply, particularly in your current role, so you can see in live terms how the concepts can work for you.

The Buoyant Leader Ecosystem

This book is part of the total Buoyant Leader ecosystem, and it links to a broader community-based set of activities. In it you will find links to our YouTube channel, kap:tv, thebuoyantleader.com, where you'll discover a whole range of support, from short video presentations across a range of topics to interviews with people who have "been there" as well as a forum in which you can raise questions and find answers to your pressing leadership issues.

And now...to begin putting forward the time-tested elements of success I have enjoyed, I will tell you a story. It is a true tale drawn from my humble beginnings as a gangly, terrified, young assistant shift manager in the airline catering kitchens of Marriott International.

Part I

The Case

Chapter 1

Aghast

Building 139 at John F. Kennedy International Airport was an imposing institutional-looking building that housed a large flight kitchen. Clad in a white lab coat, I was the young assistant manager of Marriott's in-flight services, and I oversaw a facility that produced up to five thousand airline meals a day. Now, this wasn't the peanut packet per person airline service of today. Most flights, even short hops, served a tray per passenger with some kind of hot meal, all with proper cutlery. (This was a bygone time when cleaning the plane meant emptying the ashtrays! I kid you not...there actually were smoking sections.)

Of course, with cooking and eating comes cleaning. My other responsibility was presiding over the dish room, where dozens of trucks each day would disgorge the contents of the catering service into a giant room with four enormous conveyor-belted dishwashing machines.

One sunny summer afternoon our general manager called me in to a meeting. We had a surprise visit from a fellow named George, a VIP at our single largest client, Eastern Airlines. George was a sober man with a clipped flattop military haircut and a surly demeanor. Now, I like just about everybody, but he was, well, altogether dislikable. He laid out a mystery. "We're losing our cutlery...by the thousands. It's costing us a fortune as well as delaying flights by the score. You need to get to the bottom of this and quick, and make no mistake about this: we're holding you responsible! I'm back in a week, and if it isn't solved there'll be hell to pay."

When the meeting was over, the general manager assembled his team. He made it quite clear that the mystery of this wholesale cutlery disappearance must be solved or the chaos that it produced would bring very grave consequences. As a somewhat reserved and very new member of the team, I don't know what possessed me, but I raised my hand and said, "I'll look into it." Everyone at the table seemed relieved that I, in my naive ambition, had put my head on the block. The general manager nodded, and said it would be my job to solve the mystery.

I left feeling as if I was the dog that caught the fire truck, and began by making all the necessary inquiries. I looked in our stockroom, created elaborate tracking systems for the cutlery that was in stock, and monitored all levels carefully, with no result. The losses continued.

I decided then to see whether our precious cutlery was leaking out through the loading dock, so I made a surprise visit to the dish room at 5:45 a.m., hours before the staff expected me to appear. The dish room staff worked nights so that all of the dishes and cutlery would be clean, dried, and neatly stacked for the next day's meals.

The staff was a spirited mosaic of people from places like Puerto Rico, Haiti, and all over Central America. I came to adore these endearing and at times maddening people—there were literally dozens, and I tried desperately to know each of them. Each day at the end of the shift I would see them in the cafeteria; over coffee too strong to imagine they would show me photographs of new additions to the family, ask me to help fill out their kids' college applications, and occasionally ask for a loan of $10 until payday. You haven't seen dignity until you've spent time with individuals like these, who worked so desperately hard to make a life for their families. (I was, after all, one of them, who through the miracle of a scholarship was the first in a family of laborers to go to college.)

Well, you can imagine how surprised they were to see me at such an hour. I appeared unusually businesslike as I looked through the cavernous dish room. High and low I searched and then, for some reason, as I passed the monstrous trash compactor at the end of the loading dock I looked down to see, amidst the detritus of the day's flights, gleaming Eastern Airlines cutlery.

It was being thrown away.

I turned to a knot of dish room staff and, wide-eyed, I gasped, "For God's sake, their silverware is in the compactor! It's being thrown away! What on earth are you doing?" Mr. Fuentes, the supervisor, spoke up. He looked at me sheepishly and, red-faced, replied, "Yes, Mr. Allen, we know. But it won't come clean. No matter what we do, half of it has these black stains. We run it through again and again but the stains on half of them won't go away. Mr. George from Eastern Airlines made it clear he would have our heads if the cutlery wasn't spotless at the end of the shift. We didn't know what to do. We didn't want to disappoint you." I thought immediately about how imperious I could be at times. (I shudder when I think about it now.)

So here these workers were, faced with a dilemma. They perceived that there would be dire consequences to their livelihoods if they produced dirty cutlery. The system they were working with would not cooperate and management expectations were clear, so logic prevailed. They arrived at a batch of spotless cutlery, one way or the other. The cutlery got ditched.

Now what?

Chapter 2

We'll Show 'Em

W ill you tell?" asked one of the dish room people. I scanned their faces, all looking at me in anticipation of what I would say and do next. Surely, throwing away the silverware was grounds for dismissal. I had absolutely no clue how to solve this problem. The problem, and the fault, was not theirs...it was mine.

I had to make it ours.

Looking at waiting eyes, I replied, "No, this stays with us for now, but for goodness sake, stop throwing it out and let's get to the bottom of this. I need you to help me. We'll help each other." It was then that I decided to see firsthand what an evening was like in the steamy dish room. After all, I had only encountered this group at the beginning and end of their shift. So I donned my "blues" (parlance for the light blue uniform, sort of like those you see in an operating room) and worked with them on the shift for the next week. With roaring temperatures, backbreaking work, and the time pressure of the ever-approaching end of the shift, truck after truck of messy cargoes came in, all waiting to be rendered spotless. I was shocked at what these people did in the course of their seven hours, and it became absolutely clear why—in the face of the potential to disappoint management or suffer an unforeseen consequence—they dispatched the blemished cutlery.

My mission: to reframe the task at hand. Over coffee strong

enough to walk across, I huddled in the cafeteria with some of the staff. I admitted I'd had no idea what they were up against. I apologized, but told them the issue was clear: if we didn't solve the problem, I could not predict what the man from Eastern would do. Then, in a calm and measured voice, Mr. Fuentes spoke: "We'll show him."

There was a moment of silence, and I knew in an instant that those words were a link between all of us. For me, there was a desire to prove wrong all those who thought I was too soft to lead, and for these wonderful people, there was a wish to show that they had dignity, smarts, and wanted—like me—to go home proud of what they accomplished. This was no longer me and them, it was now us.

Chapter 3

Jodell Speaks

Time after time, I heard people say that work in places like the dish room was "menial" and that the people were incapable of being motivated. Strict oversight was the recipe for performance. As the son of a construction worker, who began life among people like those in the dish room, I knew this was pure, unadulterated bunk. Everyone wants to be proud of the work they do. My grandfather always said, "Whatever you do, whether you're the garbage man or the president, work hard and be the very best you can possibly be." It was clear to me that my job as a leader was not to instruct but to help these people, who were defeated by unforgiving conditions.

As I tried to figure out what on earth to do, I could not escape the mental picture of piles of cutlery in the trash and the thought of what the rather disagreeable man from Eastern Airlines might've done if he had happened upon that sight. The inescapable fact was that, as crazy as it seems now, flights would be delayed for lack of adequate catering if enough clean cutlery wasn't available on time. So, in a strange way, the smooth functioning of the airline all came down to the dish room, but more importantly the people in blue uniforms who toiled there.

Jodell was a supervisor who managed fifty or so people who assembled the little entrées for their destination on trays to the scores of flights we catered. Diligently, workers assembled row upon row of the customary chicken, peas, and potatoes by the thousands under Jodell's watchful eye. She was old enough to be my grandmother and it was abundantly clear to everyone, including the toughest of men, that she was in charge. I liked her the moment I met her, even though she scared me to death.

Jodell was a wise woman who regularly dispensed advice in an exquisite southern accent. She took me aside. "Kevin, now don't take this the wrong way, but you and I both know you don't know your a** from your elbow but (subtly pointing to the people beavering away at the little aluminum dishes), they believe in you. It's because they know you and you've shown you care about them. Just tell them you're on their side, you know they can solve it. Keep giving them your encouragement. But for goodness' sake don't meddle, you'll mess it up for sure. They'll solve it for you, not because they've been told to, not for Marriott, or for that nasty man from Eastern; they want to solve it for *you*."

Flushed by her description of my management prowess, I knew she was right. Rather than attempting to assert a solution or to ensure that I was the unrivaled authority, I did as instructed, offering my support and belief in them, and watched as events unfolded.

Mr. Fuentes decided to enlist the help of the truck mechanics, and together they were taking a hard look at the gearing of the conveyer belts. Some of the mechanics felt that if they could slow down the conveyor, the silverware might have more time in the wash cycle. In addition, one of the staff, a plumber, was looking at the apertures to see how the chemicals fed into the hot water mix. More soap, slower conveyor... all very promising.

I realized something as I was sitting together with the workers at their breaks. We did, in fact, have a common cause. Together and individually, we had a lot to prove.

We were all striving to achieve a sense of worth, accomplishment, and recognition for our day's work. Simple as that.

Chapter 4

Told You So

"It'll never work. This is ridiculous. Let the big shots figure it out. Why should we care? We'll get blamed one way or the other anyway," said Daisy. Tall, formidable, and very outspoken, Daisy was a "catcher", the person who took clean dishes off the conveyor belt as they came through the wash and dry cycle. She intimidated me a little, but we thankfully got on well. Daisy was a cross between Eeyore and George Patton. The glass, for Daisy, was permanently half empty, and for the first time in my career I saw up close what negativity could do to an organization.

Mr. Fuentes, in contrast, was a man of few words. I am sure his people didn't know what I knew, that this deeply thoughtful father of six daughters cared and worried deeply for them. Mr. Fuentes was always the first to step forward. He was steady as we huddled together. He never let anyone know that he was anything other than certain we would somehow figure it out. At the same time, Daisy could be heard continuing her mutterings of disagreement, including how "it won't work, it won't matter," and so on. I decided it was time. Late one afternoon, I pulled her aside. "Daisy, my mom used to say that if you don't have anything nice to say... then don't say it. You know, people will listen to you, Daisy, for good or for bad. It's really for you to decide."

I walked off, leaving her to think about Mom's eternal wisdom.

The day came. The team, and our borrowed friends from the truck maintenance department, were finished with the retooling work. The dish room employees began their task. Rack after rack of cutlery was placed into the awaiting machine while the rest of us clustered at the far end of the forty-foot behemoth, waiting in anticipation for gleaming cutlery to emerge. The steam cleared...

The cutlery was still stained.

I was crestfallen. Now what?

At the conclusion of our gathering, which coincided with the end of the shift, Sal, a huge, barrel-chested Brooklynite, slapped me on the back, nearly knocking me down, and said, "Don't worry, Mr. Delightful, we'll figure it out."

Mr. *What*?

It had slipped out in the most affectionate of ways, but it was abundantly clear that I was known among the staff as "Mr. Delightful." I later deduced the nickname came from one of my many eccentricities, an arcane use of nineteenth-century language. After a sufficient number of "delightfuls" and "splendids," the name stuck. At first a bit taken aback, I realized: I was being made buoyant.

While I huddled with the team, looking over the disappointing result, Sal explained the nuances of gears and how other ideas would do the trick. I muttered, a little too loudly, "That'll fix the little thug." At that moment the entire assembly looked at me and grinned from ear to ear, clearly in agreement on my opinion of the gentleman from Eastern. It was our little secret, but henceforth the nickname "little thug" became etched in our lexicon. Now, I confess, I am not sure I was right in my choice of words, describing our "beloved" client in this manner, but, well, my working-class roots sprang forth. With those words, I unwittingly identified a powerful unifying external force—a villain, shall we say—that could keep the team focused on the task at hand and determined to "defeat" the forces aligned against them. George, wherever you are, forgive me, but it worked like a dream.

Chapter 5

Whodathunkit?

"Well, now what?" said a young member of the dish room team, with a tone of anxiety in her voice. "George comes back in two days and you know what he said. There'll be hell to pay." Together, now routinely over coffee in the cafeteria, we met to regroup. Sal and Mr. Fuentes spoke first about looking again at the gearing problem. Jodell engaged and encouraged everyone. And then the discussions were halted with two words from the most unlikely source.

"Baking soda," Daisy said, shocking everyone at the table. "My grandmother used to say that baking soda would take the paint off a Chevrolet. I tried and sure enough I got a whupping from my grandfather to show for it." We all, of course, laughed a good deal at Daisy's "misfortune." I was taken aback by how, only a few short days before, Daisy had had nothing constructive whatsoever to say. Now I could see she had joined the team.

Everyone immediately saw the wisdom in her idea. Sal jumped in right away. "Mr. Delightful," he said excitedly, "oil change pans, those large flat ones we change oil with. We can lay the cutlery out flat and fill it with baking soda." Daisy, rolling her eyes and taking charge, replied, "Well, honey, you need to know the right mixture of baking soda and water. You get the pans, and you just leave the baking soda to me."

At that moment everyone at the table scattered, some running for the truck maintenance unit and others following Daisy like chicks as she marched headlong for the supply room. Jodell and I lingered a while at the cafeteria table and she looked at me with a little smirk over the whirlwind we had inspired.

When Jodell and I entered the dish room, the floor was strewn with a dozen huge plastic bins heaped with cutlery, over which Daisy's brew had been poured. At her instruction, we let it soak overnight. The next day, we assembled at the mouth of the dish machine, Daisy with her hands on her hips, and Mr. Fuentes and Sal at the other end. We looked at each other and Jodell said casually, "Well, here goes nuthin'." And in an instant, the conveyor was loaded with our hopeful passengers. "Well, let's just see what we have for the little thug," she smirked.

Then came the wait.

The conveyor turned at a snail's pace. The cutlery made its way through a shower of water, then was rained on by detergents. Then it went to the steam and rinse. Piercing the steam and the noise came a voice… "Hey! Mr Delightful! Fugetaboudit! Who's better than us!"

The cutlery was sparkling.

The team let out a roar and Daisy hoisted me, taking my breath away, and spun me clear around. Jodell stood by, shaking her head from side to side with a glow like I'd never seen before. I have seen many things in my career: victories, corporate leaps, business achievements, elections won, but never, and I mean never, have I seen faces like those of these wonderful people in their moment of triumph. No one deserved it more.

Standing near me as the conveyor discharged one gleaming row of cutlery after another, Jodell whispered, "Told you they'd help you…." Then, with extra emphasis, to needle me, "… Mr. Delightful."

Part II

A Course in Buoyancy

Exercise 1

The Hero

> Buoyancy is a phenomenon whereby, as a leader, you float, because the people you have inspired believe you should. They believe in you because you have understood, connected with, and ignited the deep desire that lies in their hearts.

Once Upon a Time

My formative years at Marriott led me to the bare-knuckled world of advertising giant McCann Erickson. While learning the ropes of international advertising from one of my mad men bosses, I noted a sign on his desk:

Mike's Two Rules of Management:
1. Do what I tell you or else.
2. See rule number 1.

I thought the sign was one of those "You don't have to be crazy to work here, but it helps" novelties. But I realized quickly as I came to know Mike, and indeed McCann, that it was the summary of an organizational reality. McCann was the dominant leader in its field, a perfect reflection of a supply economy, distribution-based organization. The philosophy was best described to me by a wonderful man and mentor of mine Gene Kummel, once former head of the mighty McCann Erickson advertising network, during one of our many breakfasts at his spot at the Yale Club in New York. He spoke of the early days, in the 1950s, of McCann and its cornerstone account, Coca-Cola. "The CEO and I flew around the world. The CEO of Coke would go to the biggest family in the host country and ask if they would like to establish a Coke bottler franchise, then I went to the second-biggest family and asked them if they wanted to sponsor a McCann agency. Our empires grew together."

These twinned giants created a vast distribution network, dots on a map doing the bidding of the headquarters. As I took my first role as an international account manager, my new boss, Mike, explained how creating global advertising for brands like Coca-Cola worked. He told me that we created the advertising centrally in New York and then exported it to one of our dots in the far-flung McCann Erickson network of nearly two hundred offices, which operated in support of Coke's bottler network. Each office was then told that its job was to make a local version according to the exact specifications of the advertising that we sent. No deviations. In an attempt to learn how to navigate in this system, I asked Mike, "Well, what happens if one of the dots doesn't do what we want them to do?" "Look at it this way, kid," he said, pointing to his sign on the desk. "Think of us as the Roman Empire. If a province decides to revolt, we'll send the legions and burn their villages down!"

Welcome to the supply economy.

Yes, Sir

The supply economy was a well-ordered world. There were a small number of products, a few large companies that distributed them, and lots of consumers. There were a few television stations and other media that broadcast advertising telling us to buy, and buy we did.

The companies were run using a time-tested leadership method borrowed from our military cousins, command-and-control hierarchy. We executives were in charge, made it clear what we wanted, and told our people through a clear, linear chain of command what was to happen. It was even codified in a 1951 book written by William Whyte called *The Organization Man*. Communications and directives flowed downward and the only thing the organization man said in return was, "Yes, sir."

A Symbolic Demise

This orderly but slightly terrifying management system worked well for a very long time. It met its demise, in my view, when the mighty Coca-Cola Company decided to introduce an exciting new product.

In 1985, marketing history was made. I am certain, though, that no one expected history would turn out quite like it unfolded. Coca-Cola, it seemed, had been testing a new formula—one that in consumer taste test studies not only beat "old Coke," but also bested archrival Pepsi by a mile. So, presto! New Coke was heralded in advertising created by McCann Erickson featuring Bill Cosby, Coke's ubiquitous spokesperson. All anticipated that supply economy rules would apply, and they waited for New Coke to fly off the shelves.

In a mere few days, U.S. consumers were in virtual revolt. Millions of customers were up in arms, racing for the remaining old Coke available and, more importantly, expressing their extreme displeasure. People across the country, on news stations and on street corners, howled for justice. In the hallways of McCann it was rumored that a letter by an indignant consumer to Coke's CEO opened with this:

"I believe in three things: my country, my church, and Coca-Cola. How dare you take it from me?"

Whether or not the letter is apocryphal, the sentiment was certainly clear. Coke represented more than a fizzy drink—it was something people believed in and felt *they* owned, not some far off corporation. This was a watershed moment, not only in consumer marketing but for corporations at large. We were now on notice that the people really in charge were the customers. They could no longer be told what to do, when to do it, what to accept, and what to follow. They, and only they, would decide what they wanted.

A Shot Across the Bow

The New Coke debacle is especially remarkable because it involved two of the most powerful companies of the era; Coca-Cola and its advertising partner McCann Erickson were two unrivaled giants that called the shots around the globe. The event sent shockwaves rippling through business-to-consumer industries, and all woke to the new realities. We no longer dictated like we did before. A new sheriff was in town, dictating new terms: communities of people, or brand citizens, as I call them, were now calling the shots. The people we had taken for granted and labelled "consumers" were now irrevocably in charge. It was a moment that told us supply economic structure and, by extension, the leadership practices that went with it, were changed forever.

May it rest in peace.

This event was a milestone in the steady and inexorable march toward broad-scale democratization of the consumer marketplace. Through advancements in technology, this trend is leading relentlessly toward what is now called the demand economy: an economy and society where individuals are firmly in charge.

Leadership, Demand Economy Style

If "crispness of orders" and "rigor of command chain" were the key words for leadership in the supply economy, then "empathy" is the word of the demand economy. People on your team will dedicate themselves and accomplish amazing things when they see that you believe in them with your whole heart. Your primary interest is with your people. People judge whether or not they will follow you by your genuineness and your authenticity. The days of a "ruling distance" from your people—maintaining a sort of managerial omnipotence—are dead and buried.

As a sense of ownership has been tilted on its ear, so, over time, has management practice. Contemporary and successful organizations are no longer hierarchies ordered through rigid systems of command and control. Rather, they are communities of like-minded people mobilized through shared values, culture, and a collective desire. The objective of the leader in this era is to create a movement, a following of people toward a special objective. The way to do this is not through "imposition." It is through what I call *buoyancy*.

Buoyancy

Buoyancy is a phenomenon whereby, as a leader, you "float," because the people in the community you have inspired believe that you should. They believe in you, support you, celebrate your strengths, and shore up your weaknesses, all because you understand, connect with, and ignite what lies in their hearts. Creating a following requires a fundamental understanding of your audience's collective desire and an ability to mobilize it by capturing their imagination with a special quest—a common ambition and resulting culture that binds them as one.

Buoyancy means that everyone must be with you willingly, as a community, rowing together toward a common destination.

Buoyancy is a management philosophy based on a dedication to and focus on the spiritual and functional well-being of the people who will help you grow. Buoyancy rests on the assumption that everyone is different and special. You will be supported if they know you love them and believe in them, and if they feel they are part of an inclusive culture. They will compensate for your weaknesses and shore up your strengths.

You float because they believe you should.

So, How Do You Float?

Buoyancy is a process of understanding the collective desire of your people and of connecting that desire with your ambitions, beliefs, and ability to ignite them. Each person in your organization makes a decision about whether to buoy you up after they have assessed your authenticity, empathy, and connection with their true desire. In my first book, *The Hidden Agenda*, I shared what I had learned over decades of pitching for my supper—that behind every decision, of any kind and about anything, lies an unspoken visceral emotional motivation. Once you uncover and connect your genuine self to it, you have the power to win anything you seek.

Leadership is not a matter of, "I tell you what to do, then, you do it." It is a human game achieved by unearthing the deep, visceral, often unspoken desire of your people and connecting yourself to it. Leadership is the means by which you create your following and, in time, buoyancy.

People make you buoyant because you have reached them. They see you authentically and recognize that you truly understand them. With everyone's best interests at heart, together you have struck a common course. The *hidden agenda* comes in three forms: *wants, needs,* and *values.*

Wants

The hidden agenda of *wants* is based on ambition. It reflects confidence and a view of what the future might bring.

Needs

The hidden agenda of *needs* is based on fear and a desire for something that is lacking. It is a feeling of longing.

Values

The hidden agenda of *values* is centered on a person's deeply held beliefs. This hidden agenda will inevitably be directed by a value system the person holds close.

Your Leverageable Assets

Uncovering the hidden agenda of your people is step one. The next is connecting your *leverageable assets* as the means to ignite them. These assets are: your *real ambition,* your *credo,* and your *core.*

Real Ambition

This is the human desire to create something good where nothing before existed. It is a measure of your organization and of your worth. *Real ambition* is a key reason that people will follow you.

Your Credo

Your *credo* is your belief system. It is the values and principles that set you apart and guide what you believe and, most importantly, how you behave.

Your Core

Your *core* is your essence, the special abilities you possess at the center of your being. It is the special gift you have been given that separates you from others.

The Allen Key

You create the conditions for buoyancy when you connect one of your leverageable assets to the hidden agenda you have uncovered. Each of your leverageable assets is a means of unlocking one of the three elements of the hidden agenda, and the Allen Key is a tool to assist you in making these connections. Yes, I borrowed the term from my toolbox; it's a special tool for special tasks. I'll explain how it works, with examples from companies and individuals I have come to know and admire.

The *real ambition* connects to the *wants*, because it is a vision shared by you and your audience of what the future will become. You are joined because they see that their ambitions are possible with you.

The credo connects to *values*, because it is a belief system you and your audience share. You are joined because you understand them.

The *core* connects to the *needs,* because it is something special you have that solves what your audience lacks. You are joined because they see you have the solution.

Protect, Explore, and Inspire

I am one lucky fellow. A very dear friend of mine arranged an introduction to the amazing Angela Ahrendts of Burberry. I had always marveled at the way this lady—who, like me, hails from humble beginnings—rose to become one of the world's most celebrated CEOs. She managed to transform Burberry's venerable brand into one that is hot and contemporary yet maintains deep roots in its heritage. Snatching the company from the abyss of a serious, almost irreversible, decline, Ahrendts and her amazing team created a real ambition: to create a truly global luxury retail brand digitally focused for the twenty-first century. Her passion and audacity captured the imagination of her team and have ignited her people to dizzying heights.

What fuelled this passion was the intensive examination her team made of the essence—the core—of the Burberry brand. In looking deeply at the brand, the team uncovered the principles of the founder. Thomas Burberry was a maker of garments for adventurers who went out into the world without fear of the elements (thanks in no small measure to the technological advancement of fabrics developed by Burberry). Not just the fabric, but the spirit of the community of producers and proud wearers, captured the essence of Burberry, hence the wonderful words, inspired by their founder "protect, explore, and inspire". This core of capability was re-imagined by Ahrendts and her team, and is central to the contemporary branding of the company.

This platform has been galvanized by the credo of an individual—Angela Ahrendts—who believed in the business not as an organization but as a community with a profound culture, a culture that values intuition over rigidity, passion over caution, and humanity over structure. Value's she has inspired. She took my breath away our meeting, and typified the profile of a buoyant leader; thoughtful, intuitive, empathetic, and people centric but also laser-focused, decisive, and purposeful. What a treat.

The Cutlery Mystery

When confronted with any organizational challenge, whether it is problem solving at a point in time or bringing about wholesale change over the long haul, the instinct for many in charge is to dictate terms. I have to confess it often seemed easier to figure out a solution and then tell everyone what it is you want. Of course, no one is omnipotent or capable of solving all problems brilliantly. Every leader needs their people to not only help understand the problem in the first place but to participate willingly and creatively in solving it. My instinct, when I saw silverware gleaming in a trash compactor, was to immediately mete out some form of punishment. And yet, as I listened to Mr. Fuentes and the team explain, much to their embarrassment, that they could not satisfy management's demands, my heart immediately went out to them.

Empathy is a vital first step in creating buoyancy.

It is essential that you take a moment to understand the broader context your people face and decide how you are going to set out on a journey to connect with them. I shudder when I think of how close I came to a rush to judgment, but I'm so very glad that I took my moment. Jodell, I thank you.

In a Nutshell...

Creating a following as a leader requires that you have a fundamental understanding of your audience's *hidden agenda*—their collective desire—and that you connect your ambitions, beliefs, and abilities to ignite them.

Reflection

In "The Case of the Missing Cutlery," what is the hidden agenda of the dishroom staff? What leverageable asset did I use to connect with them?

Task: Applying the Allen Key

Examine your organization or one you admire—or maybe even one you are interviewing with! Study the individuals across the company. Ask yourself:

Which of the three hidden agendas is at work? *Wants,*
   needs, or *values*?
What is the collective hidden agenda?
What do people working in the organization seek?
What keeps them up at night?
What do they long for?
What do they hope to become?

Action

Now, imagine you are the leader of the organization you
chose. Ask yourself:

How would I connect with the hidden agenda I
   uncovered?
Which of the three leverageable assets do I possess that
   would ignite their desire?

Exercise 2

The Quest

> *Real ambition* is the means by which you galvanize your following. It is the driving force behind the culture you create and the motivation for your people to make you buoyant.

"Will Be..."

"We are going to make the city of New York safe for people to live the life of their ambitions." These words, intoned by a former U.S. attorney, just-defeated mayoral candidate, and now law firm partner, made our quest clear. The assembly, one I had the privilege to be among, was a small advisory group meeting in the Third Avenue law offices of Rudy Giuliani. I may not have been alone in my feelings about how impossible this ambition seemed, given a city out of control—this was wholly two years before Giuliani's second attempt at the mayor's seat. In fact, these words were the seeds of New York's Renaissance and expressed the very heart of any quest: a real ambition.

Real Ambition

Buoyancy starts with a special kind of quest: a *real ambition*. Numbers, facts, or figures do not motivate people. Rather, people are enchanted when they have the chance to create something extraordinary and when they can see clearly the opportunities they have to participate. Real ambition is the engine of any endeavor, it's the creation of something good that didn't exist before. Establish it, enlist for it, and fight for it and you'll achieve whatever you seek for yourself and for the people who will make it happen.

A real ambition is a picture of an exciting future that will mobilize the people who follow you. As you codify this desire for your future, remember that real ambition is not a *hope for*, it is rather a *will be*. It has these characteristics:

Noble Intentions

The real ambition must serve an overarching goodness. It must be of benefit to all constituencies, both inside and outside the organization. The real ambition appeals to the core in all of us that wishes to be part of creating something special.

A Statement of Clear Intent

Real ambition is not a destination or a "hoped for" goal. It is a statement of unequivocal intention and certainty of purpose that cascades to all corners of the organization.

A Seemingly Impossible Goal

Real ambition is not about increments or percentage points. It's about a great leap to a completely new state of being and, most importantly, a positive air of certainty that it can be done. People are moved when they know they are creating something special and that the real ambition is not a far-off dream but an ironclad certainty.

We Will

The simplest way to think about a statement of real ambition is with these two powerful words: "We will." With the mental picture you create, beginning with these two words, you'll change history, for yourself and your organization.

A real ambition is based on igniting a human desire. You may be setting out to save the whales, but there's no prize if none are saved. The notion of real ambition has two important parts: real and ambition.

Ambition is based on drive, focus, and a will to attain something. It has elements of competitiveness, a streak of blinding will, and a vocabulary that has one word: win. But, a real ambition is so much more. It is creating something amazing that didn't exist before.

I celebrate the long-awaited and wise recognition of the vital importance of emotional intelligence in business. This recognition represents a tectonic shift toward people not as assets but as catalysts. In this new era, achievement comes not through a chain of command but via an ignited community, which is why I use the word *real*.

Real modifies *ambition,* giving it a noble purpose. Real ambitions are the things that fire people up to get out of bed in the morning and wait with anticipation for that six o'clock conversation. Believe me, it's not percentage points or bar charts. Everyone wants to be part of creating something special, and real ambition helps you achieve that quest.

Horseshoes and Hand Grenades

Early in my days at McCann I was pursuing an account when, after a protracted struggle, the client told me we'd come in "a close second." Disappointed but pleased with our performance, I reported the result to my mad man boss. He listened and then, in his usual grumbling out of the corner of his mouth, said, "Kid, let me tell you something. Almost winning is of no consequence. Almost is good in only two things: horseshoes and hand grenades...if you get close it still counts. In business you can't almost win anything."

He was right. In my job at The Interpublic Group, a vast marketing communications holding company, driving growth across dozens of companies, I saw how organizations could settle into an acceptance culture. I firmly believe you don't have to breed an Enron culture to win, but you do need to communicate that nothing less than achieving your real ambition will do, and that accomplishing established milestones is absolutely vital. Recognition and reward for winning both small and big steps must be part of the process. It is important also to recognize that, while trial and error is paramount and a culture of experimentation is the mark of an innovator, everyone must recognize that winning is the prize.

The Mental Movie

Putting words to the real ambition is essential but can be daunting because its articulation seems crazy and overly audacious. Real ambitions I was involved with, including "We will make the city safe" and "We will redefine marketing communications," sounded preposterous; these statements seem so bold as to be embarrassing on one hand and potentially overconfident on the other. Worry not, this kind of audacity and language are absolutely essential.

In your mind there is a picture of an outcome. It is currently held in the recesses of your mind as a sort of fantasy. It's an exciting, emotionally rewarding thought. When I was searching for my first job in advertising my mental picture was this:

> *I am sitting in an office the size of small bowling alley and an elegant lady with a crisp British accent brings me tea; on the wall are clocks telling the time in various time zones of the world.*

Now, if someone were to ask me my career objective I wouldn't dream of sharing this picture, for I'd be too embarrassed. Looking back now, in fact, this was my real ambition:

I will have a position of influence at the largest and most famous multinational advertising company in the world, whose importance, reach, and scope are unparalleled.

I am proud, yet humbled, to say I achieved my real ambition. But I am still waiting for that tea…

So, what is your real ambition? What's your mental movie?

Do this exercise with your organization. Put your team together and have them express their mental movie. It's a lot of fun, allows confidence to soar over concerns, and lets audacity reign. Once you have done this, deconstruct the mental pictures to create your organization's real ambition statement.

No Calibration

One of the key defining moments in crafting a real ambition occurs as you stare at the "We will" statement you have made. It's likely that you will immediately begin to think about all that stands in the way or how utterly impossible the statement seems. This is the fork in the road: one path says you believe in the statement, the other leads you to calibrate a less ambitious outcome.

Real ambition is not about practicality. In fact, it must be entirely devoid of practicality. What would've happened to these famous endeavors if the planners had calibrated?

We will put a man on the moon in this decade.
We will make an airplane that flies from New York to
London in three hours.
We will create a drug therapy that stops HIV from killing
people.

Be bold. Be confident. Let nothing stand in your way. Identifying and sharing a real ambition is the first and vital step. It will only come to fruition if you and your people possess one very important thing: a profound sense of urgency.

Urgency

A highly important element to build in your account team as a fuel to achieve your real ambition for what you wish for your future is a sense of urgency. The best example I can think of was inspired by my seeing one of my favorite cousins Brian, at a recent wedding. Brian is a New York City firefighter. If you've ever walked past a firehouse when the truck bay door is open, you'll see the boots and the overalls carefully placed in rows near the fire truck, all awaiting the possibility of the outbreak of fire. Brian observed, "There are long stretches of boredom, but it's always in your mind…we deal in life and death." They all possess an unbending and unflinching sense of urgency.

Of course in our day-to-day corporate life, it is very, very difficult to achieve a level of urgency such as this. But believe me, urgency is the ultimate motivating force, so one of your goals as a buoyant leader is not only to establish a real ambition that can rally your organization to achieve your real ambition, but to create a sense of urgency that not a moment must be lost in its achievement. The real ambition itself is only worthy if it's attached to a vital time pressure or a moment in time to accomplish. When Brian and his team leave the fire house when the bell rings they know there are lives to be saved and not a moment to lose, so similarly, having a sense of urgency inside your organization to achieve the real ambition you have set is a means to keep the real ambition ever on the minds of your team.

Urgency is the ultimate motivating force. The saving of lives is at the highest level of urgency, and in these instances people are capable of extraordinary feats. For most of us, though, the tasks we undertake seem comparatively mundane. But must they be? Can we not harness this instinctive drive to act for a noble purpose and the greater good, and mobilize our people to achieve the near impossible? To do this, we must put to use the principles of urgency. The noble purpose is itself most crucial if it is tied to a vital time pressure, a moment in time at which it must be accomplished. The fire fighters who leave the firehouse as the bell rings know there are lives to be saved and that there isn't a moment to lose. Building a sense of urgency inside the company to achieve that real ambition is an essential part of outlining the journey that you and your colleagues are embarking on.

We'll Show 'Em!

At Marriott, I had unwittingly galvanized the dish room staff's real ambition when I invoked the challenge to show George from Eastern Airlines what we were really made of. The hidden agenda of my team was simple: to be seen as worthy. The fact is, it wasn't just them; I felt motivated, too. I yearned to prove that I could lead and achieve something for all to see; for the workers' part, in spite of their position in the sweltering dish room, they longed to show that they were resourceful, smart people who cared about doing something important. We were bound together and they floated me willingly in the name of a real ambition that would be apparent to all. It was clear that we were not just capable of achieving something significant . . . we demonstrated that we were special.

At the end of the day, people feel pride when they feel worthy. The self-esteem that psychologist Abraham Maslow described in his hierarchy of needs is a yearning every living human being possesses, no matter what kind of work she does, including working in a dish room at hundred-degree temperatures. I believe people can revel in their pursuit of a quest, providing they believe in the worthiness of their effort. This essential fuel—a belief in the worthiness of the goal—propels all great buildings, feats of engineering, advances in medicine, and journeys into the deep recesses of the earth and the outer reaches of space.

At the core, therefore, of any leadership endeavour, is the need to paint a picture, to tell a story of the journey that you and your people will travel together. This journey is a quest to accomplish something together, something that allows each and every person to delight in themselves and, more importantly, share with those who matter most. I believe in the power of what I call the "six o'clock conversation." This is the moment when you arrive home, turn to others who mean something to you, and enthusiastically say, "Guess what we did today?"

In a Nutshell...

Establishing a *real ambition* and creating your *real ambition statement* galvanizes your team and represents the first steps toward buoyancy.

Reflection

In "The Case of the Missing Cutlery," what was the real ambition of the dish room team? What was my real ambition? What did I do to galvanize the team around its real ambition?

Task

Looking at your organization, ask yourself the following:

> What is the group's higher calling?
> What real ambition do they seek?

Using the "Will be" statement as the cornerstone, write a compelling real ambition statement for your team.

Share the statement with some of the members of your team. What did they think of it?

Action

Hold a session with your team. Put the real ambition statement before them. Work through to an agreement on your collective real ambition.

Exercise 3

The Followers

> Creating your following requires a careful enlistment process that begins by inspiring your catalysts and converting your resistors.

My First Meeting

Having been awarded my first serious management job at McCann Erickson, with the remembered admonition that I would be "dinner conversation" at my employees' homes ringing in my ears, I met my new "reports." There were six of them, and two were old enough to be my parents. My mind raced. I assembled all of the collective learning that I could. I pored through the accepted wisdom set forth in management texts. What would Peter Drucker say? What about Theodore Levitt? Maybe I should throw out quotes from a general or two about "taking that hill," or perhaps "closing ranks" or "ever into the breach!" Maybe I could borrow some words from a famous football coach.

Then again, I knew absolutely nothing about sports.

The answer came in the strangest form, from the most unlikely place. That weekend as I visited my family I shared my fears. My mother spoke up, "It's simple, give them your love." Ugh! I was exasperated by what seemed to be a perfectly ridiculous observation, a moment of momentary insanity.

Now, Mom is one of those people who doesn't just see the glass as half full, she sees it as overflowing onto the table. She pursued her point, "It doesn't matter what they're doing for a living, all people are just like us—families—and every person in that family has a sense of belonging. You lead the family, and they need to know you'll care for them. They'll do things for you if they think you are genuine, and if they see that they'll follow you anywhere."

Drucker, watch out.

The Gang of Four

As you share your real ambition with a group you begin a process of enlistment. However, be prepared: not everyone will jump up and down and leap onto your bandwagon. In fact, far from it. Enlistment will be a bit of a lonely trek to start off with. It has been very handy for me, and at times quite comforting, to categorize people into four groupings: catalysts, followers, observers, resistors.

Catalysts

This is the best way I can describe catalysts: when you are about to speak to a group of people and you scan the room and see one person's eyes light up and his body language say, "I'm with you"—that person is a catalyst. Catalysts are forward-leaning, glass-half-full people. They are optimists, and they're generous of spirit. These individuals will instinctively bond with you culturally and your message will resonate with them instantly. So when you hold your first management team meeting, scan the room and look at your new team's faces—your catalysts will raise their hands, often literally. This is true not only in small gatherings but throughout the organization. Catalysts will raise their hands and make it clear they are with you.

Bring them close to you. Create "kitchen cabinets" and other work groups across organizational boundaries. This is especially helpful if you are in a position where you have a great deal of authority over large numbers of people who don't work directly for you. These catalysts will become your spokespeople, ambassadors, and stalwart defenders. Identify them, support them, promote them. In all cases, make it clear to your organization that these are the people to be emulated.

Followers

Followers are timid catalysts. They are predisposed toward you and show interest in your efforts, but would not be the first to put their heads above the parapet. They like being part of the team, not leading a team. Identifying work teams with catalyst leadership will attract followers. When you set up tasks with catalyst leaders, the followers will very quickly "sign up." They will revel in the recognition of their team's accomplishments toward your real ambition.

Observers

Observers are on-the-fence people. They are wary and want to see which way the wind blows. They don't actively work against you, but in the early stages they don't work for you either. They will need more incentive and encouragement to move toward the gathering but if they see visible success they will eventually join in.

Resisters

Like catalysts, these people are vital keys to the enlistment process. They come in two forms: the vocal objector and the passive resister. The vocal objector, like Daisy in "The Case of the Missing Cutlery," makes concerns or opposition clear early on. The person's motivation for objecting might include a rivalry for your position. Often, the resistance is based on fear and a sense of self-preservation; vocal objectors may believe that the direction you are taking will do nothing other than threaten a comfortable status quo. The good news: they are easy to spot.

Passive resisters are the real threat. They look like observers, but while smiling in assent, they quietly sow the seeds of discord. This makes observers and followers very nervous and prevents them from moving toward catalysts.

Catalyzing Your Team

The key to creating your cohesive team and beginning the enlistment process is this: identify and celebrate your catalysts; recruit and neutralize your resisters. I strongly believe, as you are finding out here, in a management principle that is not based on coercion but rather on igniting people emotionally. However, this is a not a "Kumbaya" zone. You must act swiftly and without hesitation to enlist your team in rallying your catalysts and take action against resisters. Resisters are your most potent threat and, left unaddressed, can derail your entire agenda and swing the tide of observers and followers their way.

Many leaders have told me that if they had a magic wand they would make an organization catalyze in an instant. Start by identifying each of these typologies in your organization. First rally your catalysts. Meet with them individually to get them excited about the future. Tell them you need their help. At the same time, identify and meet with your resisters. Let them know you need their support and give them a chance to air their apprehensions—their concerns may well be valid, and if you address them, these resisters might just become catalysts. In many instances, they are simply testing your mettle. The fact is, a converted resister is worth their weight in gold, as they can swing the tide of followers and observers in your direction.

If you perceive no change in the resisters you have attempted to persuade to your side, they must go. There is nothing more dangerous and corrosive than an active resister who will work against your agenda. And, by the way, such action makes it clear that you are firm and decisive about the steps necessary to ensure your real ambition. (Getting rid of such a negative force will also, dare I say, have that "Ding dong, the witch is dead" effect…)

You Set the Tone

So what can we learn about in my struggle with cutlery in the dish room? It can be found in the advice given to me by another shift manager, a wonderful man named Charlie, who would take me on his morning rounds on the production floor. He was as cool as a cucumber. He and I would be sitting in the little glass manager's office in the middle of the production floor, when he would spontaneously announce, "Oh, time to tour the orchestra."

I'd follow like a puppy as this incredibly thoughtful man glided smoothly from department to department, methodically engaging with each of the people in and around various workstations. Whether he shared a joke, asked about a granddaughter, or made small talk, he also brought, as I discovered, his eagle eye for detail, pointing out something askew or reminding the employee of something important. All in all, he was surveying the landscape of his organization to gain an intuitive feel for how each and every one of his people was feeling and performing. One thing is for sure, while all this was happening, Charlie made each of the employees feel special. Sometimes he would say to me, "Oh my, my string section is waaaay out of tune." By sheer intuition, he would know that something was troubling the folks in one of his departments, requiring him to return at a later stage.

This lesson made a big impression that I took well into my later years as I roamed the worldwide global network of McCann Erickson. Charlie's greatest comment came one morning as we came across a real screwup at one of the workstations. I was quick to point out to him what I thought the problem was and who was responsible. "Now Kevin," he told me, "you may be right, but before you go pointing a finger at them, remember that three of your fingers point directly at you. Before you go after them, ask yourself, 'What did we do, or create…or not…that contributed to these problems?'" He was so right. There was not one person among them who purposefully created a disaster; there was no one who wanted to go home and, at the six o'clock conversation, say, "Guess what I did today…I failed."

So while your first instinct might be to punish or accuse, it is vital to step back, to understand and empathize. In doing so, you'll become clear about the conditions that have been set for your people to either succeed or fail.

Cultural Permission

The other thing I admired most about Charlie is how carefully and thoughtfully he chose his words. Ever encouraging, kind, and spirited—people just seemed to light up when they spoke with him. Remember "dinner conversation?" My madman boss let me know in no uncertain terms that what I said, and how I said it, would be discussed at every dinner table of every employee in the place. He taught me that I had a vital duty to be certain that the language I used and the themes I shared would result in a positive, constructive, and motivating force, mindful always that what I said, however offhanded, would be seen as a directive— interpreted and acted upon. I call this, *Cultural Permission*.

Cultural permission is the tone, attitude, and language that emanates from the executive suite. It is a mantra, expressed in oft-used catchphrases and philosophies that move like waves through the organization. They get adopted and interpreted as actions to be followed. They become part of everyday lexicon and cultural idioms that people hear coming from the highest levels, and form a platform for what the organization believes and expects of its people. But they can be harmful and corrosive, or like Charlie, encouraging and buoyancy-fueled.

There's an opportunity for you to craft your unique language to inspire and mobilize your people. This language, carefully artic-ulated and shared, offers rich opportunities to codify and crystal-lize the sum and substance of your real ambition, your beliefs, and positive sentiments toward your people. It's buoyancy rocket fuel!

One Lucky Guy

To this day I reflect on how generous the dish room people were to me. Each of them in turn made it clear they were with me and together they set about willingly to solve the problem. At the same time, perhaps what meant the most to me was seeing Daisy, who had previously been lobbing criticisms in from the sidelines, step up to not only to offer a solution but to execute it. I have to say, I dreaded having the tough conversation with her, but bringing Daisy around had a powerful galvanizing effect—a skeptic had become a catalyst. There's little that speaks louder.

In a Nutshell...

Catalysts are the key to igniting your following. Identify them, and you'll create a chain reaction toward buoyancy. Remem-ber, at the same time do the hard work of addressing and con-verting your resisters. When you convert resisters, others will follow gladly.

Reflection

In "The Case of the Missing Cutlery," how were the catalysts recruited? What was it that brought the resister around?

Task

Looking at your organization, assign the team to each of the four categories.

> Who are your catalysts and resisters?
> Who are your followers and observers?
> Why have you categorized them this way?
> What was it about these people and their actions that made you decide how to classify them?

Action

Develop a strategy for meeting with your catalysts.

> How will you ignite your catalysts to share your vision?
> Similarly, what is your resister strategy?
> How can you draw out what troubles them?
> How can you create a shared agenda so they feel enlisted?

Exercise 4

The Setback

> Every journey has a setback. This is not an exception, but an integral part of the process. It's a test of your leadership and your team's commitment to the real ambition you have set.

People in Adversity

My grandmother used to say, "Life is happening while we're all making plans." Things will not only not go your way, at times they will seem like they are going backward. The trick is to recognize that these events are not an exception to the proceedings, but rather an inextricable part of it. You will, I can tell you now, have a setback.

At the outset, the group should be aware of the potential for reversal. When a setback is seen as a natural and expected part of the quest, it will not frighten the team, however large the impediment may be. In my early years of leading groups, I sometimes displayed excessive optimism in my desire to be highly motivating, and so faced serious morale issues when a setback finally occurred. People are a great deal more resilient than we think, providing they're crystal clear about the ambition and the collective energy required to achieve it.

As you embark on your journey, it is vital that you communicate your belief that the people with you, as they are, are capable of achieving the quest you are on. During the depths of the Great Depression, President Franklin Roosevelt set forth on a trailblazing voyage of societal and economic change to alleviate the suffering of a nation. He said, "…the only thing we have to fear is fear itself." Roosevelt instinctively understood and brilliantly acknowledged that whatever challenge was before the American people could be surmounted. This remarkable phrase, said at a time of despair and hopelessness, is the proof that the antidote to fear is hope.

Hurricane Donna

There's no better way for me to offer an all-important lesson about setbacks than with the story of a family event I will never forget. It was September 1960. A special bulletin appeared on the black-and-white television set. Kevin Kennedy, our nightly news telecaster, came on the screen. A hurricane with winds in excess of 115 mph was working its way toward the coast of Long Island, New York. I, all of six years old, interpreted this in one way and one way only: it was headed straight for our house. I was terrified. We had what we called a "picture window," a large window frame about four by five feet with a single sheet of plate glass: food for hurricanes. In preparation, my mom, with a few ten-penny nails protruding from her mouth, boarded up the window, assisted by my older brother David. At this point, I was no longer scared, I was petrified.

The storm hit Long Island hard. We were huddled in the center of the house, the creaks inside and the crashes outside deafening. The knocking of my knees added to the cacophony. Then, at a point where we were beginning to lose it all, Mom looked at all four of us, me in particular. She said very calmly, "Look at me," pointing to her face. "Do I look worried?" We all studied Mom's usual sunny demeanor and replied, "No." She then went on, "Good. Tell you what, then. I'll make you a deal. If I start to look

worried then you can. What do you think?" We all nodded immediately and she added, "I have an idea. We may not have lights, but
we've got gas so we can cook. We've got candles too, so…let's have
a hurricane party!" In short order, with the blue glow of propane
illuminating the kitchen, our giggles and the howl of winds as our
backdrop, we had ourselves a ball.

Certainty

Enlisting a team around your real ambition is all about certainty.
Not certainty about exactly what might happen along the way, but
certainty that all will come out right and that the real ambition
you have set will happen. (Remember, "We will…") Your job is
not to prevent crazy things from happening. (They will.) Your job
is to engender confidence, even if at that moment you don't have
it. When I spoke with Mom years later, she told me she was terrified, but that she had a responsibility to us kids not to let us see her
fear and to assure us of our safety. You role is to assure confidence
in a positive outcome.

Now, your role is not to sugar coat. Mom created no illusion
about the severity of the storm. You have to be candid with your
people about the circumstances. The more honest you are, the better, but you must declare your confidence in the face of these conditions. In my time working with and observing New York City
Mayor Rudy Giuliani, he declared, amidst the shocking crime sta-
tistics and a brutally challenged city, "It [making the city safe for
citizens] can be done and will be done."

Leadership demands certainty about the rightness of your
real ambition and certainty of your belief that you will achieve it.
You are not expected to have all the answers or control all events;
your certainty comes in the form of your belief that, come what
may, you will succeed. Your people need to believe that you will
support and protect them and that all will come out well—and
they will be okay. If you believe it, they will, too.

In these kinds of circumstances, you may feel the need to appear as if you have the answer to everything. You don't. You'll make yourself crazy if you think you do. When your people recognize the climate you set for them, the confidence you have, and the focus on their well-being, they'll provide you with the answers.

The setback offers an invaluable opportunity to show your people the power of your leadership and your confidence in your convictions. In fact, true leadership is demonstrated not when things are rolling along smoothly but when crisis tests you.

Don't Worry, Mr. Delightful!

When a setback occurs, you'll find your team will take extraordinary steps to help make you buoyant. Because your team knows you have compassion for them and believe in them, they will step up in a crisis. In the cutlery case, Sal made it clear he was not going to give up. He gave the team, and me, enormous confidence when we needed it most.

The ACTION Model

Here is a helpful series of steps you can take when faced with a crisis. I call this the ACTION Model:

Acknowlege the problem. It's vitally important that everyone understands what has happened, no sugar coating. You'll be surprised just what people can deal with. People are more frightened when they are in the dark. Stay calm and put the facts out there. At the same time, be sure to declare that there *is* a solution. I heard Mayor Giuliani say on more than one occasion, "People created the problem, so people can fix the problem." They are looking to you for confidence. Remember also to put the situation in a larger context.

Consider all possibilities. Sometimes, in an effort to be seen as in control, we immediately and instinctively begin "doling out orders." The first step in a crisis is to assess the situation. Don't make knee-jerk decisions. Call your people together and get all the facts. Consider carefully all the contributing factors. Weigh the consequences of potential solutions. There is never just one reason that things go awry. There are invariably several things that conspire together.

Target the cause, not the symptoms. Identify not the symptoms but the root cause and make your decisions based on the cause, and the cause alone. We are often drawn to the obvious manifestations of the problem, but behind these occurrences lie the real issues at work. The underlying causes are invariably more complex and challenging, so often it seems easier to attack the symptoms. Inevitably, if you don't attack the root cause, you're not solving the crisis.

Inspire confidence: the problem can be solved. More than half of the battle in these circumstances is confidence. If your people believe the problem can be solved, they will attack it with audacity and with an entirely different sense of purpose than if they feel the deck is stacked against them. Let them know you believe two things: 1) the problem can be solved and is not allowed to stand in the way of the real ambition, and 2) you believe deeply in their ability to solve the problem.

Organize the right team. No one person can solve a serious problem alone, but too many people on the job can also create difficulties. In our rush to make things happen, we often immediately mobilize a large number of people to get at the problem. Consequently, there's a sense of panic, which yields chaos. Decide which talents and personalities you need to solve the problem and tap those, no less and no more. Remember that a diverse team is the most effective and creative when it comes to problem solving.

Nominate your catalysts. Identify key leaders who will drive the team to a successful conclusion. In a crisis, particularly, you need to keep your most positive people closest to you. They will carry your sense of optimism and confidence that the problem can be resolved, but more practically they will rally the rest of the team to a successful conclusion.

In a Nutshell...

Setbacks are not exceptions; they are an inextricable part of your journey. The secret is not to treat them as wild exceptions. Prepare well and be measured in your response. When setbacks come, and they will, be mindful of your real ambition and that the eyes of your team are upon you.

Reflection

In "The Case of the Missing Cutlery," how did various people handle the crisis?

Task

Think of a recent crisis or problem. Deconstruct what happened.

How did the group face the problem?
Was there a consensus or acknowledgement of the problem? How well did the group work as a team?
What solution did the team arrive at? How did they get there?

Action

Take the ACTION Model discussed in the chapter and review a recent setback, applying these concepts. Might there have been a different outcome?

Exercise 5

Reaching the Summit

> Staying buoyant means maintaining your team in a state of readiness by continually learning and seizing upon the opportunities that change affords.

Lively Dinners

"Well, George, we're enjoying a full complement of cutlery. It's all here. I must say you guys really need to get a handle on your inventory." So said our general manager to the red-faced George from Eastern Airlines. No one was the wiser about our journey, and we all laughed with glee when I told the dish room staff over our usual cafeteria table just what George's expression looked like. I thought the poor man would explode. As I reflect, I can only imagine what the six o'clock conversations were like across the team. How they must've giggled about Mr. Delightful's many phrases and especially enjoyed sharing with their loved ones how each of them saved the day.

All I know is that they, and I, felt special. Being made buoyant is one thing—staying afloat is another matter altogether. To do that requires a few tricks up your sleeve. Well, they're not really tricks, but instead habits and qualities that are fundamental for leading people.

[53]

Listening

My grandfather used to say that I was "inoculated with a phonograph needle." I was, and still am, a bit of a talker. The key requirement of a leader is being a consummate *listener*. It's funny how there are courses everywhere about speaking; where are the courses in listening? The buoyant leader listens carefully not just for the facts but for what is in people's hearts, for their deep desires, fears, and values. The buoyant leader raises his emotional antennae, just like Charlie, the shift manager at Marriott, did when he toured his "orchestra." It is vital to maintain a constant vigil and to keep an eye on the emotional barometer of your people. A command of the facts is important, but an intuitive sense of your people is vital.

Learning

I met an inspired man, Hervé Humler, the president of Ritz-Carlton. This remarkable man built one of the most envied hotel companies in existence. He was as warm and courtly as he was engaging. He spoke energetically about leading his company, paying particular attention to the power of their credo—inscribed on a card that all employees carry—and to the importance of learning: "We gather our management team around the world in the morning in every location without fail, every single day. We discuss everything. We ask ourselves what happened, what went well, what went wrong and what have we learned about yesterday so that we can be better today?" These kinds of questions require a wholesale cultural shift in which we give ourselves permission to look at our failures. That is, we have to encourage a culture in which failure is not something that should be punished or avoided all costs but a vital part of the learning experience, and something that can push the company forward.

Challenging

In the old supply economy days, we thought we had all the answers. Maybe we did at the time, but we sure don't now. I love the expression, "Insanity is doing the same thing and expecting different results." Your role as leader is to continually ask the right questions and challenge everything. And if you succeed...

Start over.

The greatest enemy of achievement is calcification. This is when your ideas, processes, and teams are frozen around what you consider to be a winning formula. As an example: I watched one afternoon from my office window as workers carefully removed the enormous Pan Am logo from its namesake building in midtown Manhattan. The Pan Am building became the MetLife building. It seemed an impossibility that a powerful, foundational company could disappear. But Pan Am didn't challenge the existing order and, no question about it, disappear the airline did. The company, like many before it, failed to constantly reinvent itself.

Readiness

When I was in graduate school—an experience I loved—the business world was still operating firmly as a supply economy, and we were told we could manage change. I even took a course by that name, "Principles of Change Management." With years of leading teams and organizations now under my belt, I can safely summarize this assertion in one good New York word: baloney.

We don't manage change anymore than Mom could manage the 115 mph hurricane winds that hurtled our way. As a consequence of a consumer-directed economy and speed-of-light technological advancement, change is not a periodic thing we plan and manage, but a daily constant. Our business lives, which had been relatively orderly and predictable in the supply economy, are now chaotic and random.

In this constant change, however, lies the seeds of success and a way of advancing your real ambition. You can, and must, place your people in *readiness to seize the opportunities change provides.* With change comes opportunity, and these opportunities are the means by which you can reach your real ambition. We at McCann Erickson did not manage the forces that caused MasterCard to review its advertising account. We did, however, place ourselves in a position of readiness to win the account—a win that resulted in the landmark "Priceless" MasterCard campaign.

The Readiness Test

So like my cousin Brian in the firehouse, there needs to be a means to be in constant readiness in the spirit of the buoyant leader's journey. I've put them together in what I call the readiness test. This test is comprised of eight key characteristics of buoyancy and one you can use both as a constant guide for you, as well as a survey you can administer to your people. It can gauge their level of readiness and help you form actions to keep them a fit, high-performing team.

> Ambition: Clarity and belief in direction and purpose.
> Alignment: The degree to which people are "signed up."
> Ability: An assessment of their ability to perform.
> Urgency: A measure of commitment.
> Empathy: Awareness of the needs of others.
> Accountability: A sense of ownership and responsibility.
> Innovation: Constant idea and new solutions
>   generation.
> Bravery: A willingness to take risks, being at ease with
>   uncertainty.

The readiness test is based on buoyancy's most important principle, the collective journey and the role people play in it and a powerful means to keep your team razor sharp.

Roots

My imperious young self was a façade that hid a terrified young man. My mask fell away quickly as a consequence of the wonderful, genuine people of the dish room. They saw right through me, and thank goodness they did. I learned the power of authenticity from people like Jodell. Leadership does not mean becoming someone you're not in the name of establishing your authority. Leadership requires you to be your true, genuine, authentic self. When you give yourself over to the people of your organization and create a culture based on your deeply held credo, craft a collective real ambition, and assert your belief in your team and their ability to succeed, you will not only float, you'll shoot the rapids.

In a Nutshell . . .

Staying buoyant is a process of maintaining readiness, challenging the status quo, listening carefully, and rethinking your assumptions, all while keeping a careful vigil over the desires of your people.

Reflection

In "The Case of the Missing Cutlery," how do you think the people of the dish room felt after the general manager's meeting with George? What do you think they told their families at dinner?

Task

Think of a recent project or initiative recently concluded.

> What did you learn?
> Was there a setback? How did you handle it?
> Were you made buoyant?
> What would you do differently?
> How will the experience change the way you handle the
>   next initiative?

Action

Take some time to look at your organization.

> What assumptions should be challenged?
> What important lessons have you learned?
> What do you think should be done going forward?

Epilogue

There are many ways I thought to sum up our time together. I hope "The Case of the Missing Cutlery" and the Buoyancy Course that followed will be an ever-ready resource to help you on the journey toward your real ambition. There is one more piece of advice I want you to take with you: persist.

Do not take no for an answer. The person you are holds a recipe for success, and no matter what stands in front of you, leap over it, go around it, or, well, just knock it over. Success belongs to the persistent. Coupled with hard, hard work, persistence is the great equalizer. In trying to find an appropriate sentiment to leave you with, I was chatting with my mom, and an hour later I got the following e-mail from her (yes, eighty-three years old and e-mailing):

The setting: Deer Park Avenue Elementary School auditorium, Long Island, New York. The players: a third grade class getting ready to perform a play, *HMS Pinafore,* a Gilbert and Sullivan classic. We see on stage Kevin Allen, age seven, playing the captain of the *Pinafore,* his voice singing the stanza *"I am the captain of the Pinafore and a right good captain too."* On cue and in response, a group of young ladies skip forth singing, *"So say his sisters and his cousins and his aunts..."* They headed straight for Kevin to dance around him, but alas, the ladies are overzealous and bounce into Kevin, sending him and his three-cornered hat flying flat to the stage floor. Oblivious to the audience before him, he simply got to his feet, retrieved his hat, stood in the middle of the now circling ladies dusting off his hat and the seat of his trousers and continued as if nothing had happened, showing at an early age that even if you knock Kevin over, be ready 'cause he is getting up again!

May the force be with you.

GET IN THE GAME!

WELCOME
— *to* —
PLANET JOCKEY

A revolutionary new online game that brings business to life.

As CEO, you have just 5 weeks to turn around
a large multinational company.

Be faced with real life decisions and dilemmas with
real consequences.

Fend off the competition, beat the media speculation,
and most importantly make your people believe in you as you
test your leadership skills to the full.

Can you take your company to the top, make it to the
boardroom showdown, and remain buoyant?

Visit www.planetjockey.com